*Primarily
Speaking:*

Learning
Activities
on the Missions
of the Church

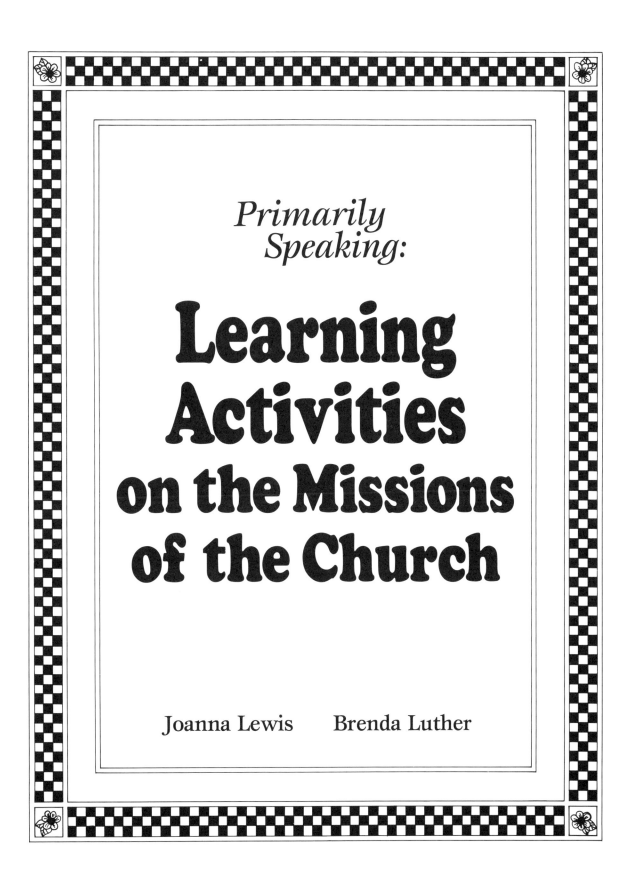

Primarily Speaking:

Learning Activities on the Missions of the Church

Joanna Lewis   Brenda Luther

Bookcraft
Salt Lake City, Utah

ISBN 0–88494–815–3

First Printing, 1991

Printed in the United States of America

DEDICATION

It has been said, "A friend is someone who walks in when the rest of the world walks out."

We want to dedicate this book to each other. We have been friends since we first met eight years ago and have often wondered if we knew each other in the premortal life.

To all others whose friendship we have cherished over the years (especially Myrna, Karen, and Diane)—this book is for you too. Friends, like families, are eternal.

The Threefold Mission of the Church

Proclaim the Gospel

Perfect the Saints

Redeem the Dead

PROCLAIM THE GOSPEL

Friendship and Missionary Work

We have had a wonderful experience putting the ideas together for this book. The threefold mission of the Church is very important, and we hope this book will help you teach children to come unto Christ.

The first section of our book focuses on proclaiming the gospel. Friendshipping less-active members and nonmembers is a very important part of missionary work. Thus we included friendshipping in this first section.

This section begins with a story and a poem on friendship. We put a new twist on an old card game and made an "Old Friend Game." The game cards emphasize the characteristics of a good friend. The little note cards located after the game are fun and can be used over and over again.

The specifically missionary-related part of this section starts out with a cute flip-chart poem that explains some things we can do to be better missionaries. There is a game that shows how fun it can be to give out copies of the Book of Mormon. The section concludes with a cute picture that any child would love to hang in his or her room.

FRIENDSHIP CLUB

"This meeting of the M&M Club is now called to order," said Melonie, the president. "What is on our agenda today, madam secretary?"

Melissa spoke up, "Today we are going to try out Marcey's new fingernail polish, walk Sister McDonald's dog, jump on the trampoline and, of course, have M&Ms for refreshments."

"That sounds great," said Melonie. "Let's get started."

Marcey, Mandy, Melonie, and Melissa had recently become the best of friends. Their families had all moved to the same street, and the girls hit it off right away. They had much in common with each other: they were all nearly the same age; they were all members of the Church; they all went to the same school; they all had baby sisters; and their names all began with the letter *M*. This was a very special friendship indeed.

Soon after the girls got to know each other, they started a club. They had a club meeting every Wednesday after school. The club had three rules:

1. All members had to be girls.
2. Each member's name had to begin with the letter *M*.
3. Each week they had to do a service project for one of their neighbors. (Mandy's mother insisted on this before she would let Mandy join.)

The club was lots of fun for the girls. In Marcey's backyard was an old playhouse that they used for a clubhouse. Their mothers helped them make some giant pillows to use as chairs, and they had an old desk for the president to sit at. The girls put some of their favorite posters up on the walls, and they even made a big sign for the outside. The sign read, "M&M Club—Members Only!"

School was finally out, and the girls were very excited to begin their summer activities. There would be swimming lessons, arts and crafts, lots of slumber parties and, of course, club meetings. They were determined to have a wonderful summer.

One day, about two weeks after school had ended, a big moving van pulled up in front of a house across the street. The girls sat on the curb with their chins in their hands, watching the men unload the big truck. They wondered what might be in all those boxes, but mostly they were curious about the people who would be moving in.

"I wonder if they have any kids," said Marcey.

"They must have a baby," said Melissa. "I saw the men taking a crib into the house."

Just then a small car pulled into the driveway. The girls all sat up and anxiously watched as the family got out of the car.

The mother got out first. She had a baby in her arms. It looked like a boy. Next the father got out and opened the back car door.

"Come on, honey," he said. "Let's go see our new home."

A young girl slowly got out of the car. She was tall and had the prettiest long curly hair the girls had ever seen.

"She looks like she is about our age," Melonie whispered.

They all watched as the new girl walked towards the house. Just then, Melissa sneezed. The girl turned and saw all of them sitting on the curb. She smiled a faint smile and shyly turned towards the house.

Melissa's face turned bright red as the girls wondered what to do next. Mandy's mother, who was out watering some flowers, approached the group of girls and broke the silence. "Would you girls like to take a pitcher of lemonade over to our new neighbors?"

"Sure!" they all said as they jumped up.

The new family enjoyed the lemonade. Moving is hard work, especially during the hot summer. The girls had a chance to visit with and find out about the new family. They had just moved from California, and the pretty, long-haired girl was eleven years old. Her name was Sara. Marcey, Mandy, Melonie, and Melissa were all excited to have a new friend.

The girls all got along great. Sara fit right in. She had a lot of new ideas for fun things to do.

When the next Wednesday rolled around, Marcey, Mandy, Melonie, and Melissa wondered what they should do about their M&M Club.

"She can't join," said Melissa. "Her name doesn't begin with the letter *M*."

"But she's our friend," said Mandy. "We need to change that silly rule and rename our club."

All the girls agreed, and Sara was asked to join their club. Sara was thrilled.

"This meeting is now called to order," said Melonie. "What is on our agenda today?"

"We are going to weed Sister Jones' flower patch," Melissa began. "Then we will make a new club sign. It will say, 'Friendship Club—Everyone Welcome!' "

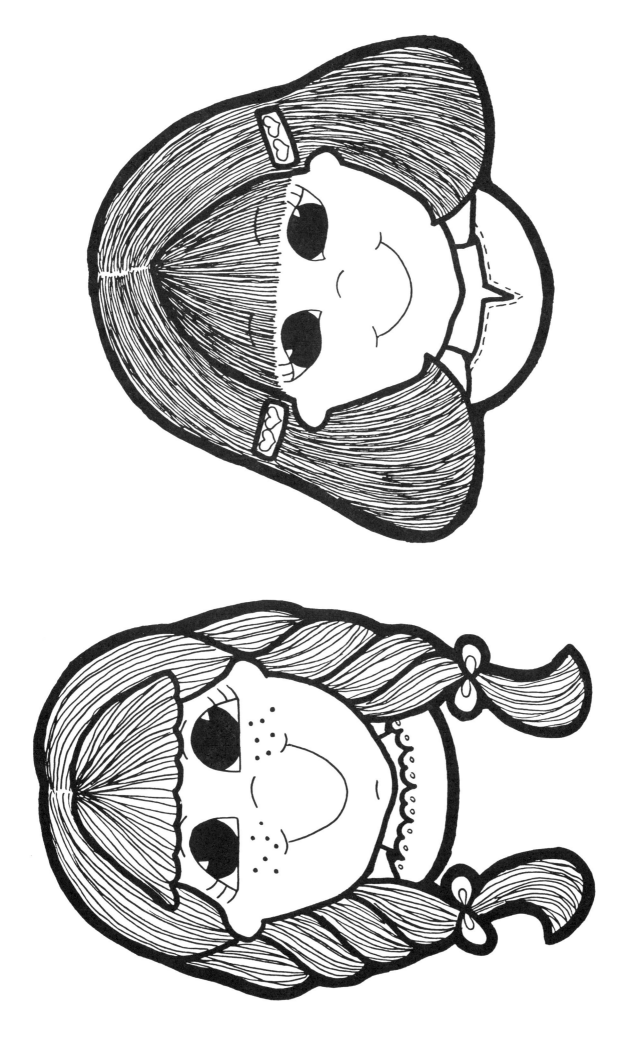

M&m Club

Members Only!

Friendship Club

everyone Welcome!

The **Moving Company**

S. S. FRIENDSHIP

Climb aboard the *S. S. Friendship*,
  It won't cost you much—
Just a smile or a handshake,
  Or maybe a gentle touch.

This ship sails on forever,
  So on its decks you'll stay,
And get to know all the passengers
  It picks up along the way.

Friends come in all shapes and sizes,
  Young or old, short or tall.
The *Friendship* never discriminates;
  It welcomes one and all.

Sometimes it sails on rough seas,
  Sometimes on calm and blue.
But whatever seas it's sailing on,
  The *Friendship* is always true.

S.S. FRIENDSHIP

Old Friend

Instructions

Game Preparation: Copy both sides of cards on cardstock, being careful to line up pictures on front and back. Color lightly if desired. (Dark coloring may show through.) Laminate and cut out.

Game Rules: Play this game the same as you play the popular card game "Old Maid," except that the person who is left with the Old Friend is the winner! Have fun!

Secret-Saving Sally

Secret-Saving Sally

Loving Louis

Loving Louis

Helpful Helen

Jolly Joseph

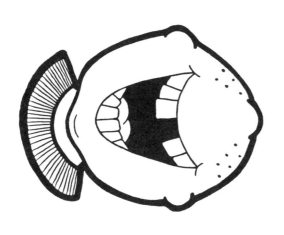

Celebrating Celeste

Helpful Helen

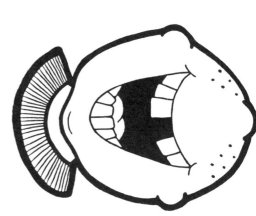

Jolly Joseph

Celebrating Celeste

Listening Linda

Listening Linda

Serving Sam

Serving Sam

Supportive Sara

Supportive Sara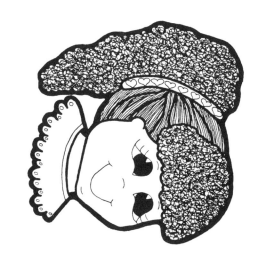

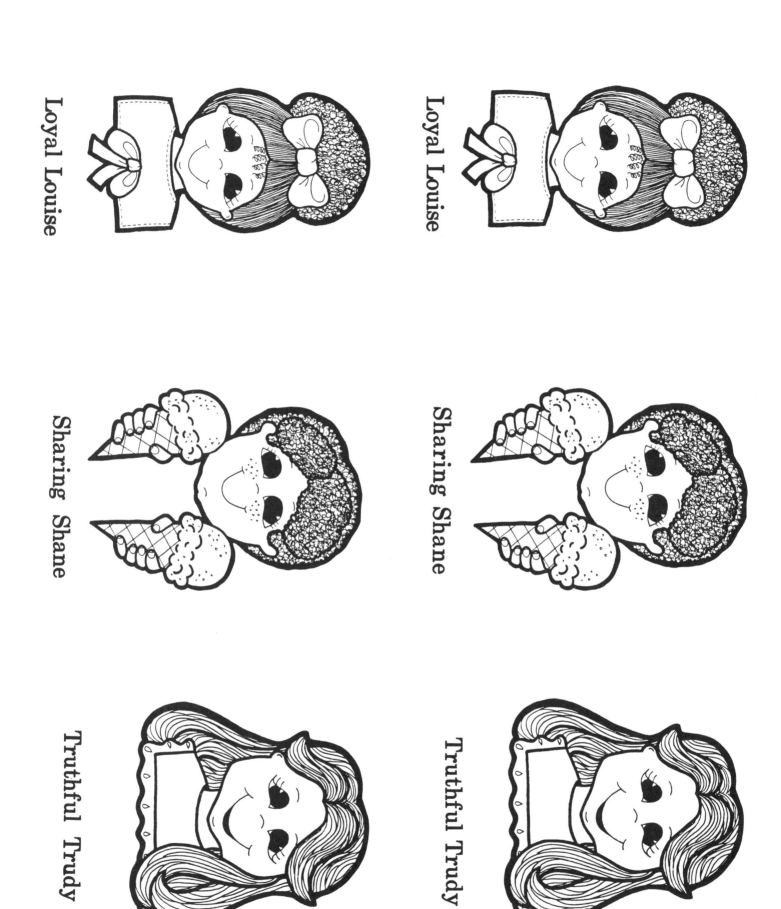

Loyal Louise

Loyal Louise

Sharing Shane

Sharing Shane

Truthful Trudy

Truthful Trudy

Appreciative Alice

Appreciative Alice

Sportsman Spike

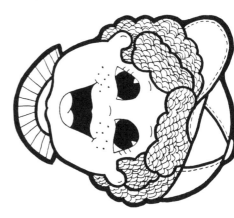

Sportsman Spike

Forgiving Fran

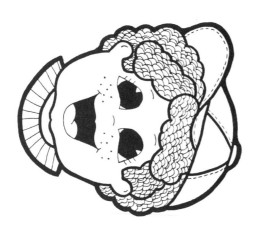

Forgiving Fran

Dependable Dan

Dependable Dan

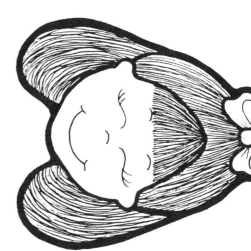

Sympathetic Cindy

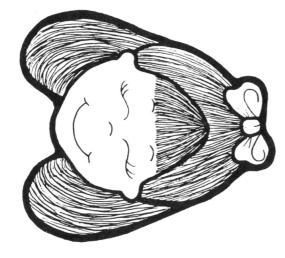

Sympathetic Cindy

Trustworthy Tom

Trustworthy Tom

Reliable Renae

Reliable Renae

Thoughtful Thad

Thoughtful Thad

Playful Pam

Playful Pam

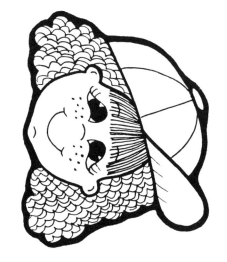

Fun Freddie

Fun Freddie

Kind Kara

Kind Kara

Caring Curtis

Caring Curtis

Ring—a—ling goes the doorbell
And away we do run.
From a special friend you know,
This yummy treat did come !

Just a note

from a friend to say,

Hope you're having

a wonderful day !!

I wish I had a miracle pill
To give you while
you're feeling ill.
Or some medicine upon a spoon
That would make you
get well soon.

The Church sends out missionaries two by two
  To teach the gospel and tell everyone it is true.
And even though we are not sent abroad,
  There's a lot we can do to teach the word of God.

Pray for guidance every night and day;
Our Heavenly Father will show us the way.

Showing love is important, maybe the most important of all,
It doesn't matter if you're old or very, very small.

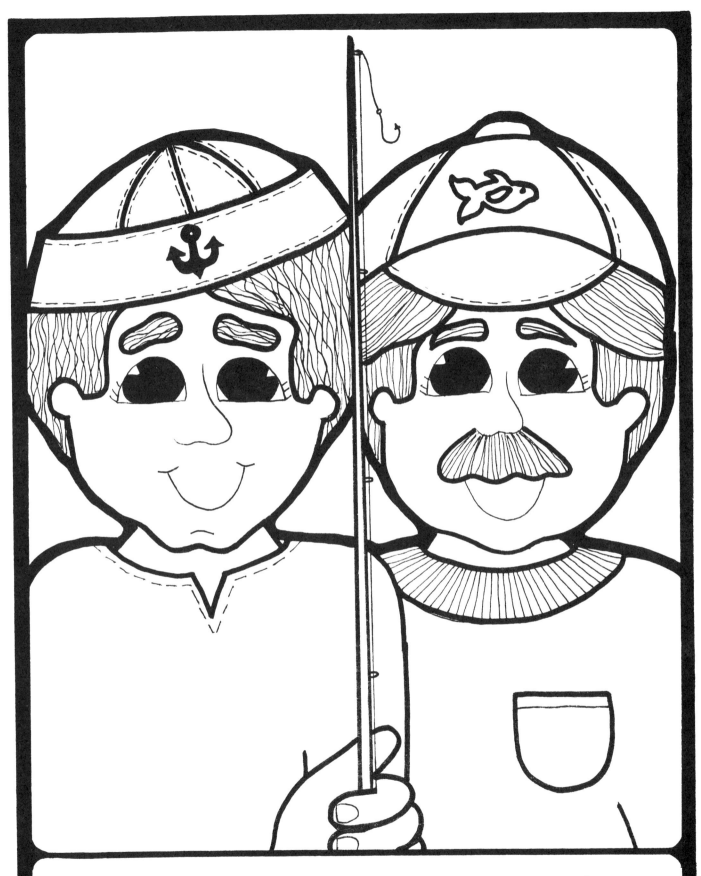

Fellowshipping others is in every missionary's book.
Showing love and kindness always gets you off the hook.

Giving out Book of Mormon copies is good to do.
Write your testimony inside. Say you know it is true!

Sharing the Church magazines with neighbors and friends
Can show others our church brings great dividends.

Invite someone to church. Just give them a call.
Say, "Come to Homemaking. We're going to have a ball!"

Serving others is great! Just give it a try.
You're going to find out it's easy as pie.

Share your testimony with someone you know.

Sharing your testimony will help it to grow.

Missionaries can be young, or they can be old;

The Lord calls them all so his message will be told.

Book of Mormon Drop

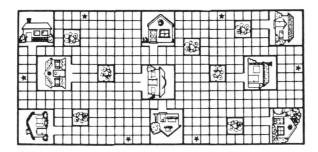

Game Board: Copy all three game board pages on cardstock. Color if desired. Cut out and carefully place together. Laminate, leaving an eighth of an inch between board pieces if you want to fold game and store it in a file folder.

Die: Copy on cardstock and laminate. Cut along the dark lines. Fold along all dotted lines. Tape together to form a cube. (Untape the cube to store with the rest of the game.)

Book of Mormon Cards: Copy the set of books below on six different colors of paper. Laminate and cut out. Each player gets a set of nine Book of Mormon cards (all the same color).

Missionary Markers: Copy on white cardstock. Color the outside borders to match the six different colors of Book of Mormon cards. Color the missionaries as desired. Laminate and cut out. Overlap the solid-lined edge past the dotted line to form a cylinder. Tape in place. These cylinders will stand up on your game board. (Untape them for storage.)

Game Rules: For two to six players. Each player takes a missionary marker and the nine corresponding Book of Mormon cards.

Each player places his marker on a star. The players then take turns rolling the die and moving accordingly. Moves may be made horizontally, vertically, forwards, or backwards, but not diagonally. If a player comes to a flower obstacle, he or she must go around it.

The object of the game is to move from house to house, dropping off copies of the Book of Mormon. Players must go through the entrance square of every house and may only leave one Book of Mormon card at each house. The first player to give out all his copies of the Book of Mormon wins the game!

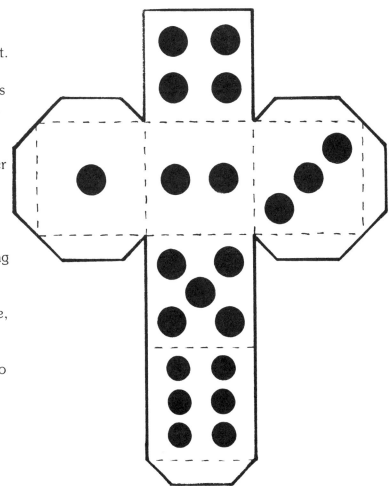

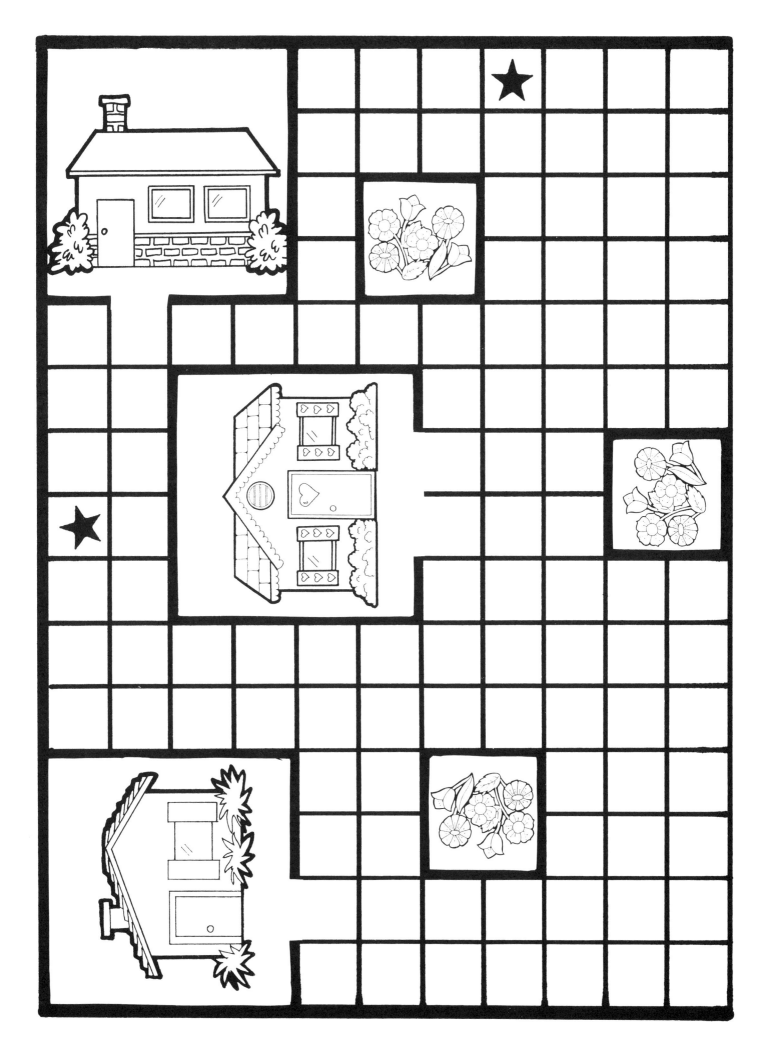

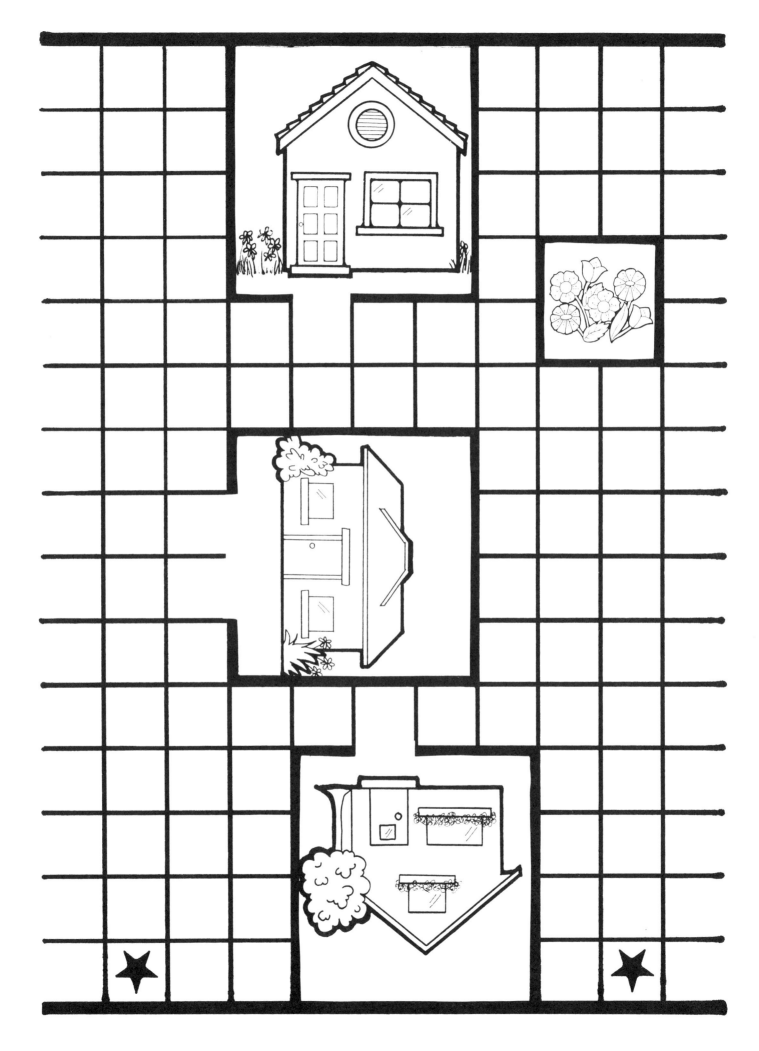

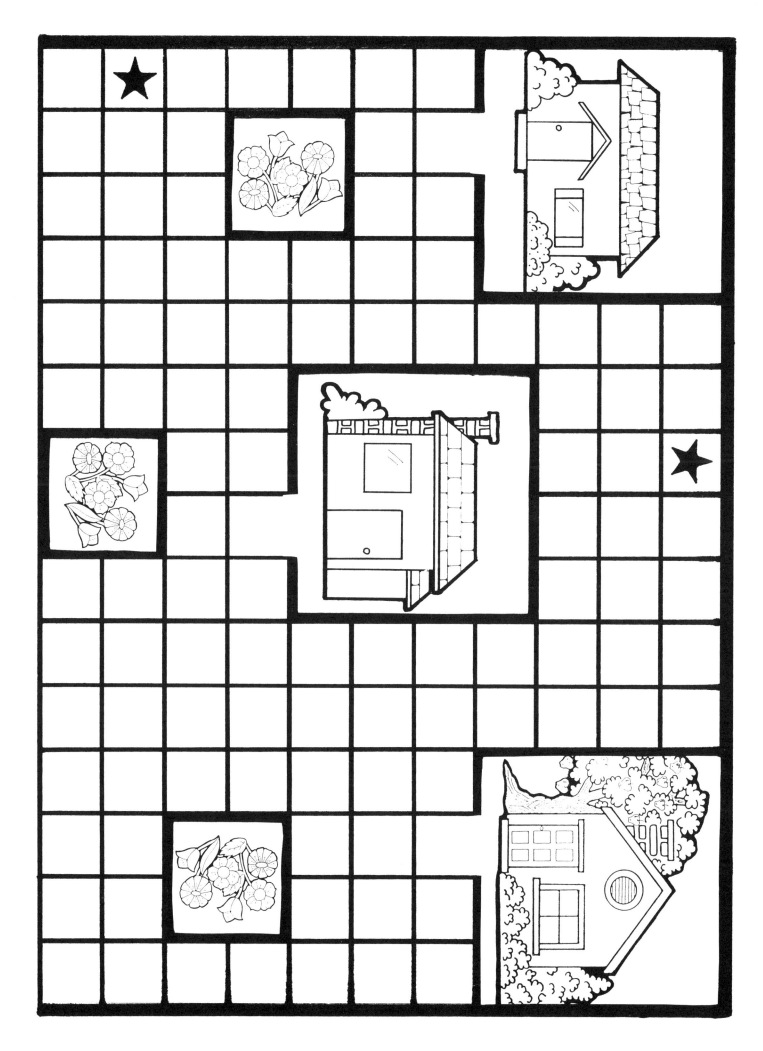

PERFECT THE SAINTS

Goals and Gospel Principles

Perfecting the Saints encompasses many things. In this section of our book we have chosen to emphasize goals and gospel principles, because they are basic parts of the Church.

In the goal section we have a fun story called "A Recipe for Life." Can you guess what the recipe of life might be? There is also a page of motivators and goal charts. These will be fun to use as refrigerator magnets or handouts to remind us how important goal setting is.

We have included a story and a fun game to help review the basic gospel principles of the Church. We hope these will be useful and fun to you. This section concludes with a gospel principles word scramble that you can copy and use as needed. Children love mind teasers like this. Have fun!

A RECIPE FOR LIFE

Jason and Sally bounded into the kitchen. They had been outside playing, when they smelled something yummy cooking and had to find out what it was.

"What are you making, Mom?" asked Sally. "It sure smells good!"

"Yeah," agreed Jason. "Can we have some?"

"I am trying a new recipe," said Mother. "It is called 'Peanut Butter Kiss Cookies,' but they're not quite done yet."

"What is a recipe?" asked Sally. She had often watched her mother cook but had never understood what all that measuring meant.

Mother liked to take every opportunity to teach her children gospel principles in ways that they could understand, and this was a perfect chance to compare a recipe to life. She was glad to have this opportunity to teach the children about eternal goals.

"A recipe is a guideline," Mother began. "It tells you what ingredients you will need in order to make something taste good. It not only tells you what you need but also tells you how much of it you will need, and exactly when to add it."

She showed the children the recipe card. Mother then explained to them what all the abbreviations meant. "It is very important that we add the exact amount of each ingredient to our food, or it will not taste very good." Mother added, "We must also make sure all the ingredients are fresh and not spoiled.

"Have you ever thought that we need a recipe for our earthly life?" asked Mother. "Can either of you think of what it might be?"

Both children looked very puzzled. They had never thought about a recipe for life before. What on earth did Mother mean? They shook their heads.

"How about goals?" Mother began. "When we set some eternal goals and write them down, they become a guideline, or a recipe, for our life."

The children looked relieved. They had been taught about goals before, and they knew goals were very important.

"You each have your own eternal goal list," Mother added. "Why don't you get them while I take these cookies out of the oven, and we can review your goals together."

The children scurried off to their rooms. Mother took the cookies out of the oven and placed a large chocolate kiss in the center of each one. The cookies looked delicious. Just then baby Nick woke up. Mother swept him up into her arms and gave him a big hug. Soon the other children were back, waving their goal lists.

"Let's have a cookie while we talk about your goals," Mother said. "You be first, Jason."

They had a nice time reading their lists and eating fresh-baked cookies. It made them commit themselves all over again to follow their own eternal recipe so that they would someday live eternally with Heavenly Father. But for now, they could enjoy kisses from the cookies and lots of hugs from Mother. What more could a child ask for?

350°   C.   tsp.

    3 1/2

    pkg.

Tbsp.

PEANUT BUTTER KISS COOKIES

1 c. brown sugar
1 c. shortening
1 c. peanut butter
2 eggs
1 c. white sugar
4 Tbsp. milk

2 tsp. vanilla
1 tsp. salt
2 tsp. soda
3 ½ c. flour

1 pkg. chocolate kisses (for garnish)

Mix all the ingredients together. Shape into walnut-sized balls and then roll balls in additional white sugar. Bake at 350° for 10 to 12 minutes. Immediately after removing from the oven, press a chocolate kiss in the center of each cookie so the cookie cracks around the edges.

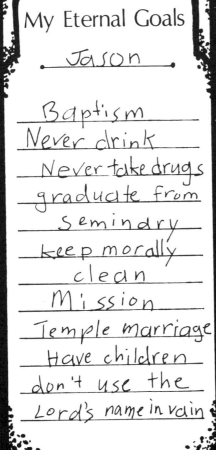

My Eternal Goals

Jason

Baptism
Never drink
Never take drugs
graduate from
Seminary
keep morally
clean
Mission
Temple marriage
Have children
don't use the
Lord's name in vain

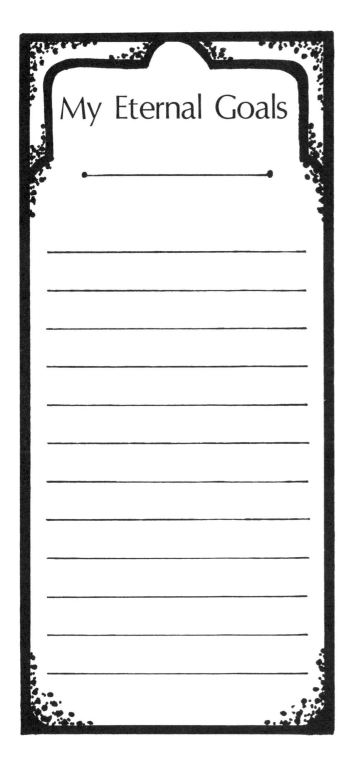

My Eternal Goals

• _____

_____

_____

_____

_____

_____

_____

_____

_____

_____

_____

My goal: _____

_____

Reaching

0 ——————————— 0

your goal

10 ——————————— 10

isn't hard -

20 ——————————— 20

If you do it

30 ——————————— 30

yard by

40 ——————————— 40

yard!

50 ——————————— 50

It takes patience to reach your goal!

FISHING FOR ANSWERS

It was a beautiful Saturday morning. Jeffery and his father had gotten up early to go fishing. They had been planning this fishing trip for weeks, and Jeffery was very excited. Mother helped them get everything ready for the trip, and soon they had everything loaded and were off for the lake. It was still dark as they drove, so Jeffery slept most of the way.

The sun was just peeking over the mountains as Father parked the pickup truck by the lake. It was a beautiful morning. The lake was so calm, it looked like a mirror. They could see a reflection of the mountain in the water.

"What a great morning!" said Father. "I'm glad we are doing this."

"Me too," Jeffery said as he rubbed his eyes.

They quickly unloaded the small rowboat and launched it into the water. Father helped Jeffery put on his life jacket, and then put on his own. They put their fishing poles, lunch, and the tackle box into the boat. They were all set to go fishing. Father held the boat steady as Jeffery got in, and then climbed in beside him.

Father rowed the boat along the shoreline for a while, and then turned towards the middle of the lake. When they were about one hundred yards out, Father stopped rowing.

"This looks like a good place to fish," he said. "Are you ready?"

Jeffery smiled excitedly and grabbed his fishing pole.

"First we need to bait our hooks," said Father. "Let me show you how to do it." Jeffery cringed as Father put the poor little worm on his hook. He sort of felt sorry for it. After he caught his first fish, Jeffery decided that worms made pretty good bait.

As they sat in the little boat and fished, Jeffery and his father had a chance to talk about school, Jeffery's friends, soccer, and a little about Dad's work. All in all it had been a super morning.

It took most of the morning to catch enough fish to feed the whole family, but finally they were finished.

"I can't wait until supper," said Jeffery. "These fish are going to taste so good! Mom and Katie are going to love them."

"Well, son," Father began, "we won't be able to eat them for supper tonight. We will have to put them in the fridge and have them for lunch tomorrow."

"How come, Dad?" asked Jeffery.

"Because tomorrow is fast Sunday," Father said. "Do you know what that means?"

"Oh, sure," Jeffery started. "It means we won't get to eat for two meals again. I can't wait until our bishop changes this fasting rule."

"But Jeffery," Father began, "our bishop can't change what you call the 'fasting rule.' Fasting, by which we draw closer to our Heavenly Father, is an eternal principle, so it can't be changed. We can fast at any time. But the whole Church is asked to fast once a month, on a Sunday, and only our prophet could change this rule.

"There are many eternal principles," Father continued. "Can you think of some more?"

As Father rowed the boat back to the dock, Jeffery named a few eternal principles. "Baptism, the Ten Commandments, and prayer," said Jeffery. "Is the Word of Wisdom an eternal principle?"

"It sure is, because it has to do with taking care of our bodies," Father said. "So are love, service, the plan of salvation, and temple marriage. As members of The Church of Jesus Christ of Latter-day Saints, we agree to follow these eternal principles. As we do, our Heavenly Father will bless us."

"I guess fasting two meals is a small price to pay for all the blessings we have," Jeffery said. "Maybe we'd better eat an extra sandwich to help hold us until tomorrow."

Father rowed the boat to a shady spot, and they ate their lunch. "Fishing is not only fun," said Jeffery between bites, "it is very educational too. Maybe next time I'll bring my spelling book!"

Father laughed as he grabbed another sandwich.

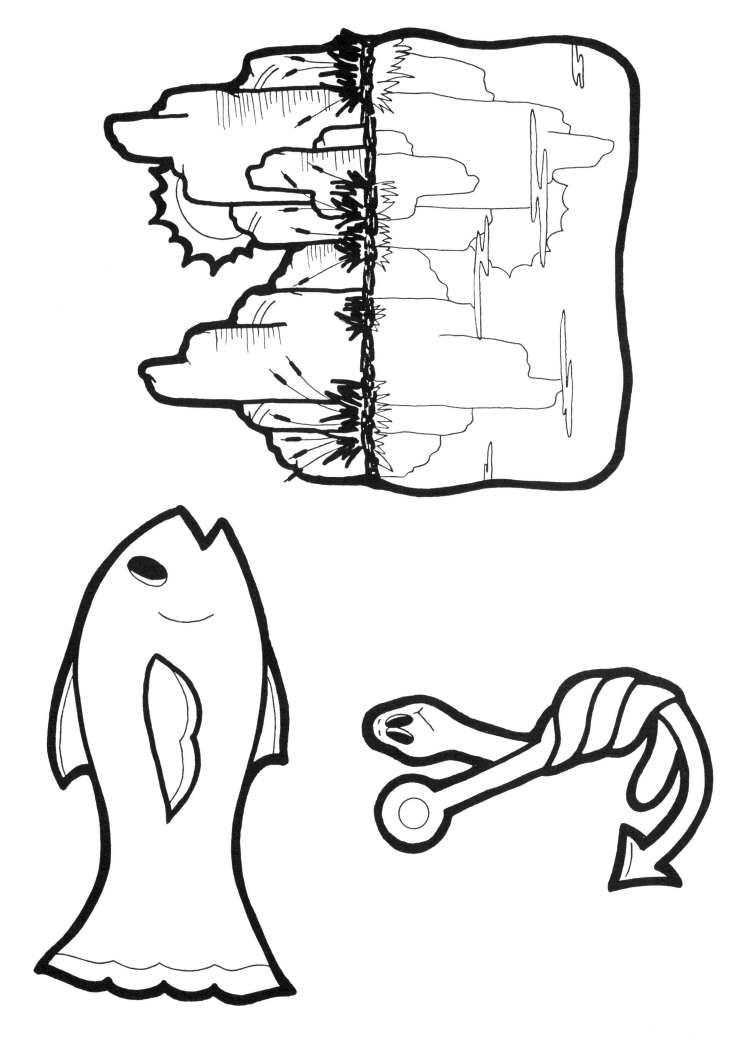

GOSPEL
PRINCIPLES GAME

Game Preparation: Copy all the pieces on cardstock. (Copy as many blank and "Repent!" pieces as you like.) Color as desired. Laminate and cut out all the pieces. Arrange the pieces on a table to form a big game board (see top of this page for an example).

Die: Copy on cardstock. Color if desired, laminate, and cut out along dark lines. Bend along all the dotted lines and tape together to form a cube. (Untape for storage.)

Game Rules: Begin on the "Start" square. The first player rolls the die and moves accordingly. If he lands on a gospel principle square, he reads it out loud and does what it says. If he lands on a blank square, he stays there and it's the next player's turn. If he lands on a "Repent!" square, he must go back to the beginning and start again. Continue playing until a player reaches the "Finish" square. This player is declared the winner!

Note: There are no markers included with this game. Use markers from another game, or use household items as markers. Also, this game can be blown up about sixty-five percent and used as a giant game board. Lay the pieces out on the floor, and each person can be his own marker. Either way, it's lots of fun!

LOSE 1 TURN

SWITCH WITH THE PERSON IN THE LEAD

REPENT!

GO BACK TO THE START

FINISH

START

PLAN OF SALVATION

You gave a lesson on the plan of salvation for family home evening.

Move ahead 4 spaces.

PRAYER

You were running late this morning and forgot to say your prayer.

Move back 2 spaces.

SERVICE

You helped your mother bake a pie for the Joneses.

Move ahead 2 spaces.

TEMPLE MARRIAGE

You set a goal to be married in the temple.

Move ahead 1 space.

TITHING

You earned $6.00 baby-sitting and remembered to pay your tithing.

Move ahead 2 spaces.

ARTICLES OF FAITH

You memorized an article of faith.

Move ahead 2 spaces.

BAPTISM

You gave a talk in Primary about baptism.

Move ahead 3 spaces.

WORD OF WISDOM

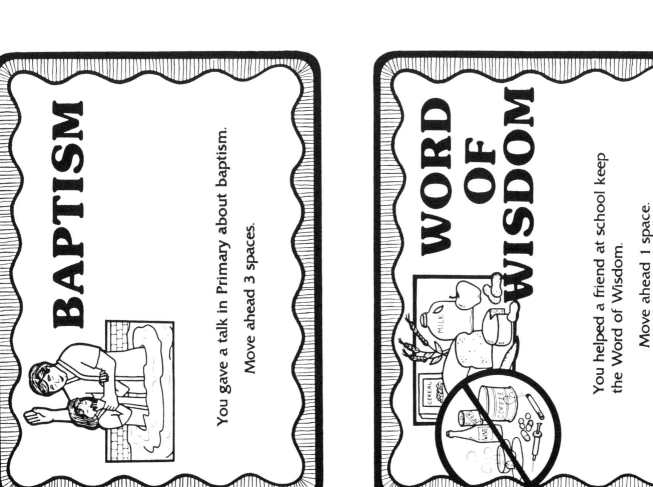

You helped a friend at school keep the Word of Wisdom.

Move ahead 1 space.

SCRIPTURES

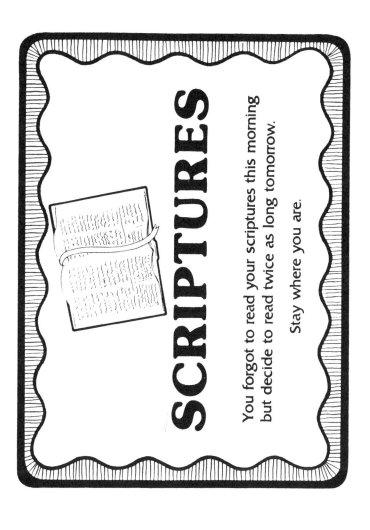

You forgot to read your scriptures this morning but decide to read twice as long tomorrow.

Stay where you are.

PRIESTHOOD

You disobeyed your father's righteous counsel; thus you didn't honor the priesthood he holds.

Move back 2 spaces.

FAITH

You bore your testimony in sacrament meeting. That shows a lot of faith.

Move ahead 2 spaces.

COMMANDMENTS

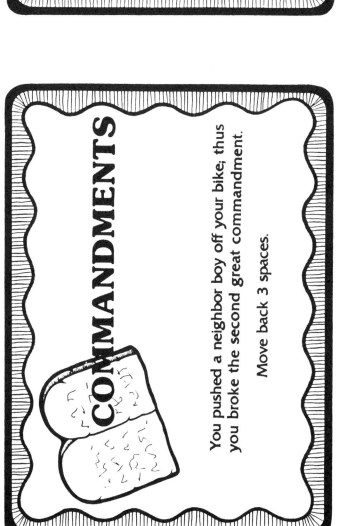

You pushed a neighbor boy off your bike; thus you broke the second great commandment.

Move back 3 spaces.

MISSIONARIES

You put some extra money in your mission account.

Move ahead 2 spaces.

SACRAMENT

You were thinking about baseball instead of our Savior during the sacrament.

Move back 3 spaces.

CONFIRMATION

You attended a friend's baptism and confirmation. The Holy Ghost testified to you that the Church is true.

Move ahead 3 spaces.

LOVE

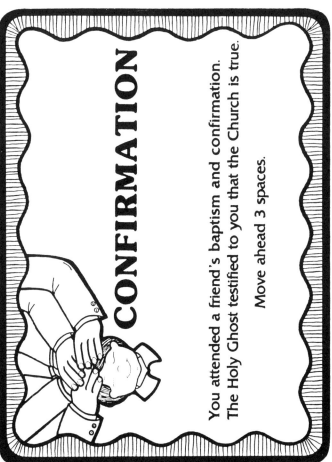

You hit your little brother, but immediately felt bad and gave him a hug.

Stay where you are.

GOSPEL PILLS

If you want to be happy the rest of your life,
And never suffer from spiritual ills,
You must follow some rules of our Heavenly Father:
They are known as "gospel prin-ci-pills."

The Ten Commandments and the Articles of Faith
Are the most basic "pills" of all.
The Word of Wisdom keeps our bodies clean;
It will help us grow big and tall.

Our priesthood "pills" run the Church;
The same as in days of old.
But without the scriptures and missionaries,
The stories would never get told.

Love and service "pills" go hand in hand,
As do fasting and prayer.
All symptoms vanish as we partake,
And we feel Heavenly Father near.

As we pay tithing—it's only a tenth—
Blessings come and we're safe from harm.
And taking the sacrament every week
Gives us a real "shot in the arm."

So we may return to our Father in Heaven
A wonderful plan He's designed.
With Jesus as Savior, and ordinances too,
Our way back to Father we'll find.

Our faith increases each time that we
Partake of a "prin-ci-pill."
As we receive the recommended daily allowance,
Our spiritual vessel is filled.

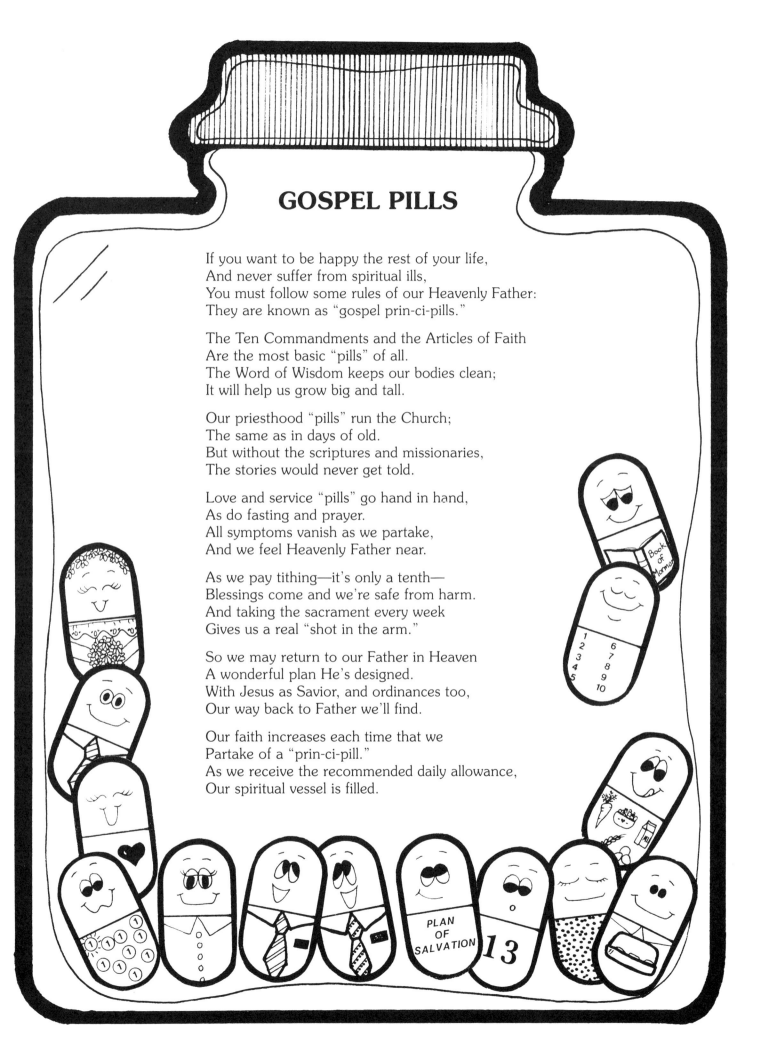

WORD SCRAMBLE

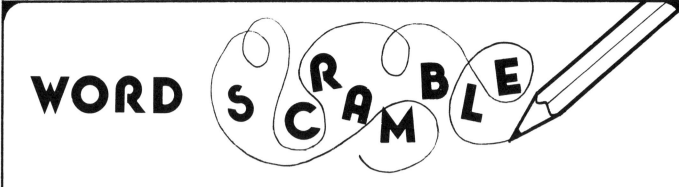

Ghititn _____   Olev _____

Cevirse _____   Thafi _____

Pitsbam _____   Yarepr _____

Tipscruesr _____

Marcnaset _____

Cepaternen _____

Fatirononcim _____

Lapn fo Vitonalas _____

Pemlet Ramirega _____

Rdow fo Somdiw _____

Cilrates fo Tahif _____

Nte Nomdetmsancm _____

Articles of Faith	Love	Ten Commandments
Confirmation	Scriptures	Repentance
Prayer	Baptism	Plan of Salvation
Service	Tithing	Temple Marriage
Word of Wisdom	Faith	Sacrament

REDEEM THE DEAD

Temples, Families, and Genealogy

In this final section of our book you will find ideas on teaching children about temples, families, and genealogy. We feel that these topics are all a part of redeeming the dead.

There are two pages of temple-related handouts that will be fun and useful. Copy and use them as needed.

Family unity is stressed next. A story about a "peachy" family teaches us the importance of family members working together. A fun game is next. It teaches us that even though each member of our family is different, all members are important. A poem entitled "Heirlooms" links us to our ancestors.

We have designed a new genealogy book to copy and use as needed. It will show your children that genealogy work can be a lot of fun. The refrigerator magnets will help us remember all our important family members.

We hope you will enjoy using this book as much as we have enjoyed putting it together!

I want to be married in the Temple.

REMINDER

Ward Temple Night

Date:

Time:

Temple Reminder

Fill in the time and date of your ward's temple night. Copy and use as needed.

Family Picture Frame

Draw or paste your family's picture in the frame. Copy as needed.

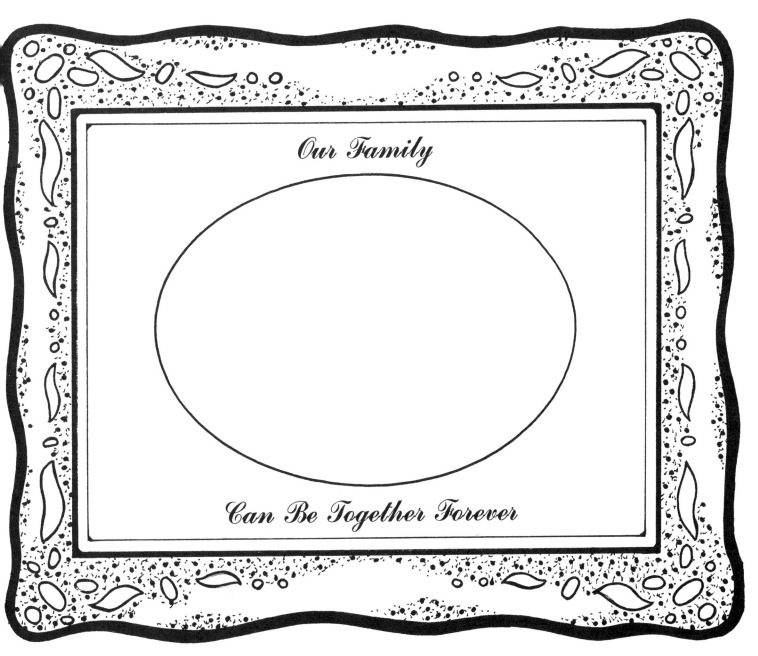

Our Family

Can Be Together Forever

A PEACHY FAMILY

Mother stood at the kitchen sink, peeling peaches and carefully placing them in the bottles. The smell of cooking peaches filled the air. Canning was one of Mother's favorite things to do. She canned anything and everything she could get her hands on. Having a good supply of food on the basement shelves gave her a sense of security.

This particular day of canning was not going quite as well as usual. The baby, little Ricky, had an upset stomach, and Mother had had a hard time getting him to take his nap. The other children weren't cooperating either. Little chores hadn't gotten done, and the two boys, Mark and Jeromy, were having a grand time teasing four-year-old Annie. Finally, to make matters worse, it was hot! Canning peaches is a hot job anyway, and the weatherman said that this was going to be the hottest day they'd had so far that summer.

Mother wiped her forehead with the back of her hand as she leaned over to pick up the third bushel of peaches. Suddenly a crash came from the living room. Mother dried her hands as she ran to see what had happened. As she hurried through the doorway, she saw her favorite lamp on the floor in a million pieces. Mother stopped in her tracks and stared down at the three guilty-looking faces. Which one should she scold first?

Just then, little Ricky started crying in the next room. Mother rolled her eyes and went to comfort Ricky, leaving the three children alone with their thoughts. Mother gently rocked Ricky, and soon he went back to sleep. Mother breathed a sigh of relief. Now, what to do about the other disaster? When she finally came out of the baby's bedroom, she calmly told Mark, Jeromy, and Annie to follow her to the kitchen.

"Sit down on those chairs," said Mother, pointing at the dinette set. "I'll be right back." Mother hurried down the stairs and soon returned carrying another jar of peaches.

"Do you children know what the word *cooperation* means?" Mother asked.

The boys could tell she was still upset, so they just nodded their heads.

"They talk about cooperation on TV sometimes," said Annie. "But I don't know what it means."

"Well," began Mother, "we are going to have a lesson about cooperation right now. Everybody better listen up!"

Mother held up the two bottles of peaches. One bottle was one she had just taken out of the canner. The peaches in it looked fresh and good to eat. But the peaches in the other bottle, the one Mother had just gotten from the basement, looked rotten. They were all brown. No one would like to eat them.

"Can you see any difference in these two bottles of peaches?" asked Mother. The children all nodded their heads. "The peaches in this bottle," Mother said, "are fresh. They will stay fresh looking and good to eat for a couple of years. But the peaches in this other bottle are rotten."

"What happened to those peaches, Mom?" asked Mark.

Mother told them that something must have gone wrong with the processing, because the jar hadn't sealed correctly.

"You see," explained Mother, "everything has to work together to make the finished product desirable. If even one step isn't done just right, the whole batch could be spoiled. I have to follow the directions carefully, add just the right amounts of ingredients, cook them for just the right amount of time, and then the peaches will turn out perfect."

The boys were starting to understand the lesson Mother was teaching. "We all need to work together too!" said Jeromy.

"That's exactly right!" Mother exclaimed. She was glad that the children were getting the message. "When even one of you doesn't do your part, it can spoil things for the rest of the family. When we all do our fair share, the work is easier and we have a more desirable home. This is called family unity!"

"We can have a 'peachy' family!" said Annie with a smile. The boys and Mother started laughing.

"Becoming a unified family is something that your father and I work very hard for," Mother said. "Only by working together can we become a celestial family, and that is our ultimate goal on earth."

Just then, Father came home from work. He noticed that the lamp in the living room was broken and that the rest of the house was more than a little messy. He slowly walked into the kitchen and heard Mark apologizing for breaking the lamp.

"How was everybody's day?" asked Father.

With a twinkle in her eye, Mother said, "Peachy, just peachy." She winked at the children and they all burst out laughing.

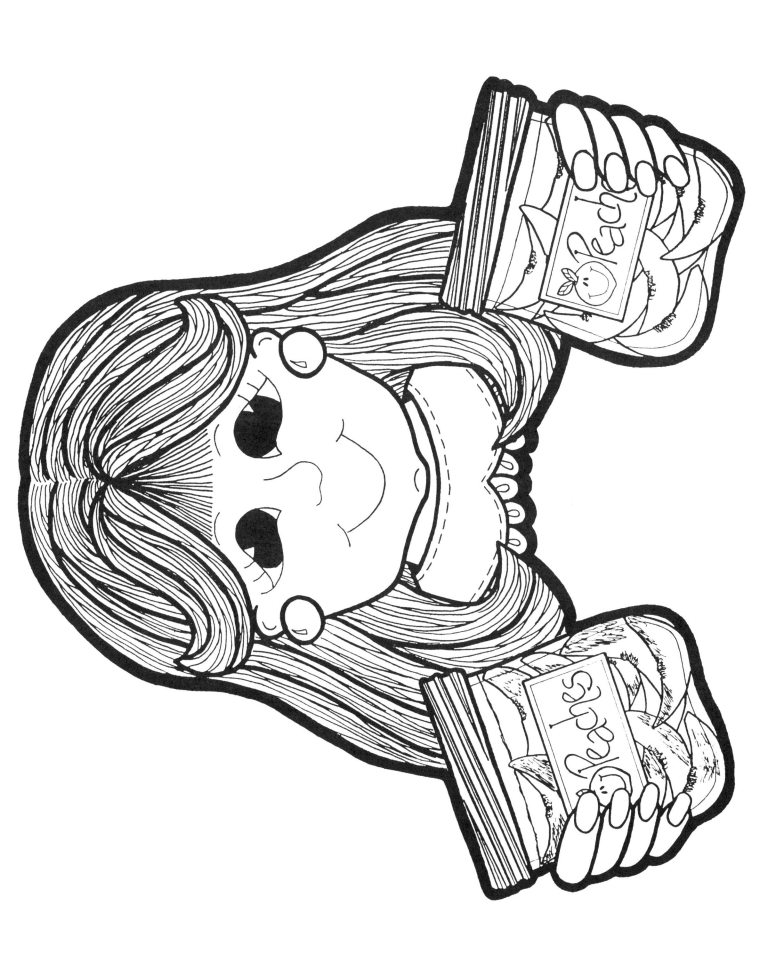

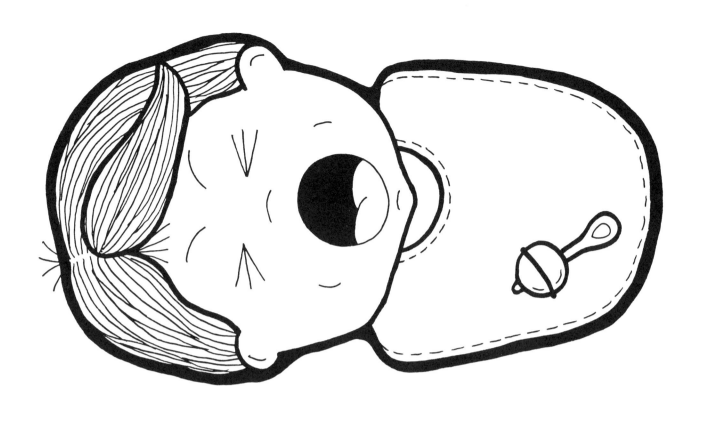

Game Preparation: Copy all pages on cardstock. Color as desired. Laminate and cut out all pieces. The two pages of small cards name some of the ways family members differ. They are the draw cards.

Game Rules: This game is for three to eight players. It is played much like bingo. One person is the caller. He picks one of the draw cards and reads it out loud. The rest of the players check to see if they have the particular family trait on their "4-Some Family Fun" cards. If they do, they cover it with a bean or a penny. The first person who gets four in a row wins the game. Trade cards and play again. A blank card is included on this page, for those who need more cards.

BOY

BROWN HAIR

MUSICAL

LEFT-HANDED

BLUE EYES

LOVES ANIMALS

GOOD ARTIST

BLOND HAIR

WEARS GLASSES

GREEN EYES

BROWN EYES

MUSTACHE

LONG HAIR

YOUNG

GIRL

DIMPLES

FRECKLES

OLD

4-SOME FAMILY FUN!

BROWN EYES	**GREEN EYES**	**LONG HAIR**	**FRECKLES**
FREE	**OLD**	**MUSTACHE**	**LEFT-HANDED**
 **GIRL**	**LOVES ANIMALS**	**GOOD ARTIST**	**MUSICAL**
WEARS GLASSES	**BROWN HAIR**	**BLOND HAIR**	**BROWN EYES**

4-SOME FAMILY FUN!

FREE

LOVES ANIMALS	 DIMPLES	YOUNG

BOY	WEARS GLASSES	GIRL	GOOD ARTIST
BROWN HAIR	OLD	GREEN EYES	BLOND HAIR
MUSICAL	LONG HAIR	MUSTACHE	FRECKLES

4-SOME FAMILY FUN!

LOVES ANIMALS

BROWN EYES

FRECKLES

DIMPLES

GOOD ARTIST

BLUE EYES

BROWN HAIR

LONG HAIR

BLOND HAIR

FREE

MUSICAL

GIRL

BOY

WEARS GLASSES

YOUNG

OLD

4-SOME FAMILY FUN!

GREEN EYES

WEARS GLASSES

BROWN HAIR

BOY

LOVES ANIMALS

GOOD ARTIST

BROWN EYES

FRECKLES

MUSTACHE

LEFT-HANDED

MUSICAL

LONG HAIR

BLOND HAIR

BLUE EYES

DIMPLES

FREE

4-SOME FAMILY FUN!

BLOND HAIR	OLD	DIMPLES	YOUNG
WEARS GLASSES	BOY	FRECKLES	GIRL
LEFT-HANDED	BROWN HAIR	LOVES ANIMALS	GREEN EYES
BLUE EYES	MUSICAL	FREE	MUSTACHE

4-SOME FAMILY FUN!

OLD	BLUE EYES	BROWN HAIR	GREEN EYES
GOOD ARTIST	MUSICAL	LONG HAIR	MUSTACHE
LOVES ANIMALS	DIMPLES	YOUNG	FREE
BOY	FRECKLES	BROWN EYES	LEFT-HANDED

4-SOME FAMILY FUN!

DIMPLES

YOUNG

MUSTACHE

LEFT-HANDED

FRECKLES

GREEN EYES

FREE

BLUE EYES

OLD

GIRL

BLOND HAIR

LOVES ANIMALS

LONG HAIR

BROWN EYES

WEARS GLASSES

BOY

HEIRLOOMS

My mother has a curio cabinet
    That's full of all kinds of stuff—
Things my mother says are precious,
    That we are *not* allowed to touch.

She calls them family heirlooms,
    Trinkets from days gone by,
Things our ancestors passed down
    To remind us of their lives.

There's some brightly colored china
    That belonged to our Great-Aunt Sue.
She used to throw grand parties,
    And would use that china of blue.

My grandmother's round white doily
    Sits upon the second shelf.
Grandma taught Mother to make them,
    When Mother was only twelve.

The glasses Great-Grandpa used to wear
    Are sitting there tarnished and old.
But Mother thinks they're "oh so grand!"
    She wouldn't trade them for silver or gold.

There are five pairs of tiny shoes;
    The ones which we children wore
When we were newborns long ago—
    Tiny babies our mother adored.

Many things sit upon those shelves:
    Pictures, my dad's first train,
A vase with rosebuds on the front,
    And a necklace with a pretty gold chain,

Some pillowcases, a jewelry box,
    My mother's high school ring,
Our large book of remembrance—
    Mom says it's the most important thing.

There are many more things in that glass case,
    Things both precious and dear.
Seeing them there reminds me that
    Our ancestors are ever near.

GENEALOGY

My Genealogy I've just begun,
But I'm finding out it's lots of fun!

This special book belongs to:

_____

This is my Pedigree Chart
of people who are dear to my heart!

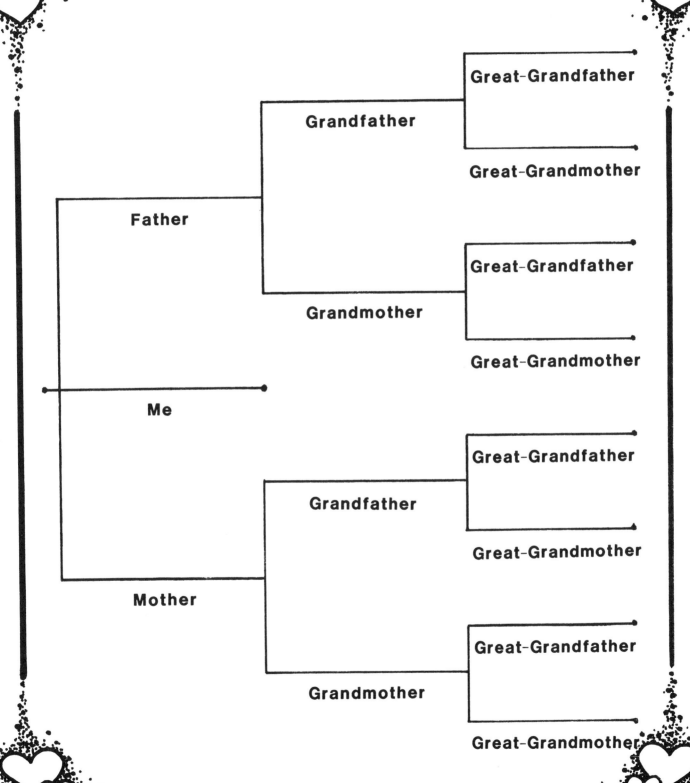

Father

Grandfather

Great-Grandfather

Great-Grandmother

Grandmother

Great-Grandfather

Great-Grandmother

Me

Mother

Grandfather

Great-Grandfather

Great-Grandmother

Grandmother

Great-Grandfather

Great-Grandmother

I may be young, but each year's been well spent.
I'll record for each one a special event!

12

11 ♥

10 ♥

9 ♥

8 ♥

7 ♥

6 ♥

5 ♥

4 ♥

3 ♥

2 ♥

Age 1 ♥

Birth

All about my MOM

Full name: _____

Birth date and place: _____

_____

What were some of your feelings on your wedding day? _____

_____

_____

How did you feel when I was born? _____

_____

All about my DAD

Full name: _____

Birth date and place: _____

_____

What was your first job? _____

_____

How did you meet Mother? _____

_____

Gathering information
            is fun to do,

So I conducted a
        personal interview!

I talked to: _____

This is what I learned: _____

_____

_____

_____

_____

_____

_____

_____

_____

These are some important dates: _____

_____

_____

_____

I have ancestors
who really cared;
They kept a history
of stories to share!

Here is one of my favorites: _____

_____

_____

_____

_____

_____

_____

_____

_____

_____

_____

_____

_____

Family Favorites!

Paste or draw pictures of your family.

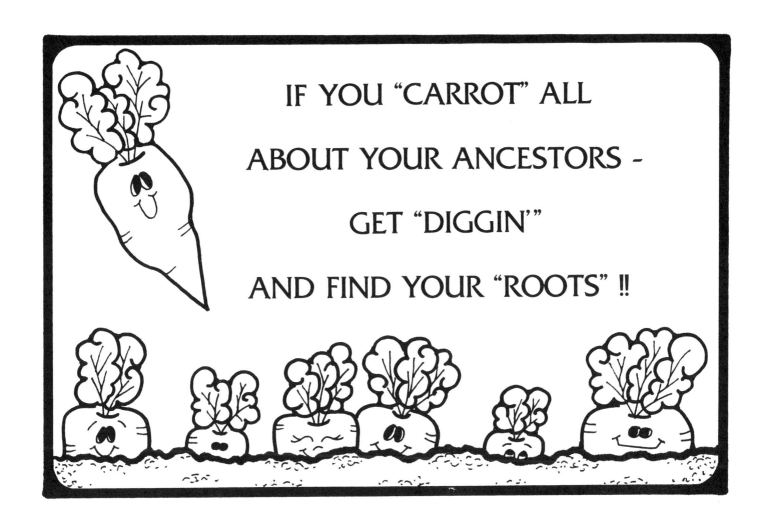

IF YOU "CARROT" ALL

ABOUT YOUR ANCESTORS -

GET "DIGGIN'"

AND FIND YOUR "ROOTS" !!

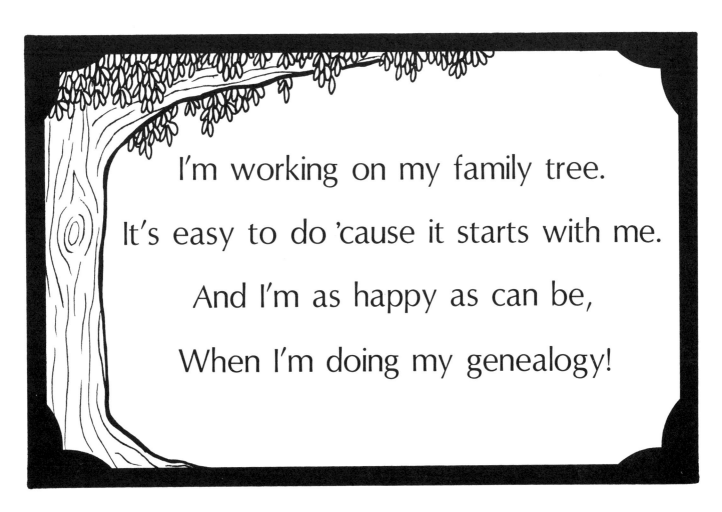

I'm working on my family tree.

It's easy to do 'cause it starts with me.

And I'm as happy as can be,

When I'm doing my genealogy!